UNITED NATIONS CONFERENCE ON TRADE AND DEVELOPMENT

Technical and statistical report

From non-tariff measures data to impact

Guidelines for the analytical pathway from non-tariff measures inventory to trade impact assessment

United Nations
Geneva, 2025

United Nations Publications
405 East 42nd Street
New York, New York 10017
United States of America

Email: publications@un.org
Website: https://shop.un.org

United Nations publication issued by the United Nations Conference on Trade and Development

UNCTAD/DITC/TAB/2025/4

ISBN: 978-92-1-159601-4
eISBN: 978-92-1-154582-1
Sales No. E.25.II.D.43

Table of contents

List of Tables

List of Figures

Acknowledgements

This document was prepared, under the overall guidance of Ralf Peters of the Division on International Trade and Commodities of UNCTAD, by Denise Penello Rial, with non-tariff measures and trade data provided by Fabien Dumesnil and Rado Razafinombana.

Desktop publishing and design were undertaken by Jenifer Tacardon- Mercado.

Chapter I

Introduction

Introduction

Non-tariff measures (NTMs) play a crucial role in shaping international trade. While tariffs remain important instruments of trade policy, NTMs increasingly play a prominent role in determining market access and trade costs. According to UNCTAD (2024), NTMs tend to have a significantly greater impact on trade costs than tariffs.[1] Thus, NTMs may – even unintentionally – act as barriers to trade. Moreover, they often serve legitimate public policy objectives, such as protecting health, safety and the environment.

Unlike tariffs, which are relatively straightforward to quantify—typically expressed as a percentage of the product's value or in monetary terms—NTMs are inherently more complex. They encompass a wide range of regulatory measures, including product requirements, health and safety regulations, and import quotas, whose trade effects are not easily measurable. Their administration is often fragmented across multiple government agencies, further complicating transparency and analysis. Tariffs are more transparent, as countries generally publish and communicate their tariff schedules to the public and World Trade Organization. As NTMs continue to grow in importance, understanding their nature, incidence, scope, implementation, and impact on trade is essential for policymakers, researchers, and stakeholders engaged in global trade.

This guideline presents possible analytical approaches used to support policymakers in understanding and designing regulations that minimize costs to trading businesses while maintaining important public policy objectives. This document focuses on methodologies that can be used to assess the impact of NTMs on trade and development.

This quantification analysis can only be done using suitable data, highlighting the importance of transparency on NTMs. For this purpose, it is essential to use and maintain a database that applies a standardized approach for data collection across economies and through time, such as the TRAINS database.[2] Transparency can be achieved through notifications or active data collection such as the World Trade Organization (WTO) trade policy review. UNCTAD and its partners complement these approaches and maintain a structured NTMs database suitable to be used for quantitative analysis as well as direct qualitative and quantitative information.

The UNCTAD TRAINS dataset has the following characteristics:

- **Coverage.** The UNCTAD TRAINS database represents the most comprehensive global repository for NTMs information, compiling official regulations from about 150 economies, representing more than 95 per cent of global trade. The data

[1] Quantitative analysis of the data shows that NTMs are more costly than tariffs. The trade weighted average of AVEs is about 4.7 percent and the simple average 8.1 percent. UNCTAD (2024) provides the probability distribution graph of the AVEs. Reasons include that tariffs have been reduced over decades until the end of 2024 in trade agreements as well as unilateral decisions while technical requirements became more and more demanding.

[2] The data collection methodology and classification used is well documented in past UNCTAD publications.

covers all requirements that can potentially affect international trade for a specific product in a specific economy and for a specific trading partner at a specified point in time.

- **Methodology for data collection.** The collection approach is standardized and described in the Guidelines for Collecting NTMs; the latest version was published in 2023. NTMs are recorded in a neutral way with the purpose of fostering transparency of the policy tools that may affect international trade. There is no *a priori* judgement that they constitute barriers, even if they may have an impact on trade.
- **Source data.** NTMs data in the Global TRAINS NTMs database stems from legal national requirements that can directly or indirectly affect international trade in goods. Only official regulatory information is used for populating the database.
- **Granular level information.** NTMs data is published as easily accessible data in TRAINS online with systematic information about the regulations and measures. The measures are classified using 4-digit NTM codes according to the International Classification of Non-Tariff Measures. Each measure found in the regulations is linked to the specific product list –at the HS6 digit level– to which the legal requirement is applied, as well as the trade partner that it applies to.

The database's comprehensive coverage, detailed content and granularity enhances transparency and enables statistical analysis and economic research.

The NTMs data user guide UNCTAD (2024) describes the data collection approach and how to access and use the NTMs data that are publicly available in the TRAINS database. This report follows this user guide and focuses on the process of analysing NTMs data. It provides further description on the structure of the database, highlights common misinterpretations, and discusses how descriptive data can inform policy considerations. In summary, this document presents the statistical uses of the data, focusing on the methodology for impact quantification of NTMs on trade and development.

Chapter II

From NTMs data to trade impact analysis: A logical sequence

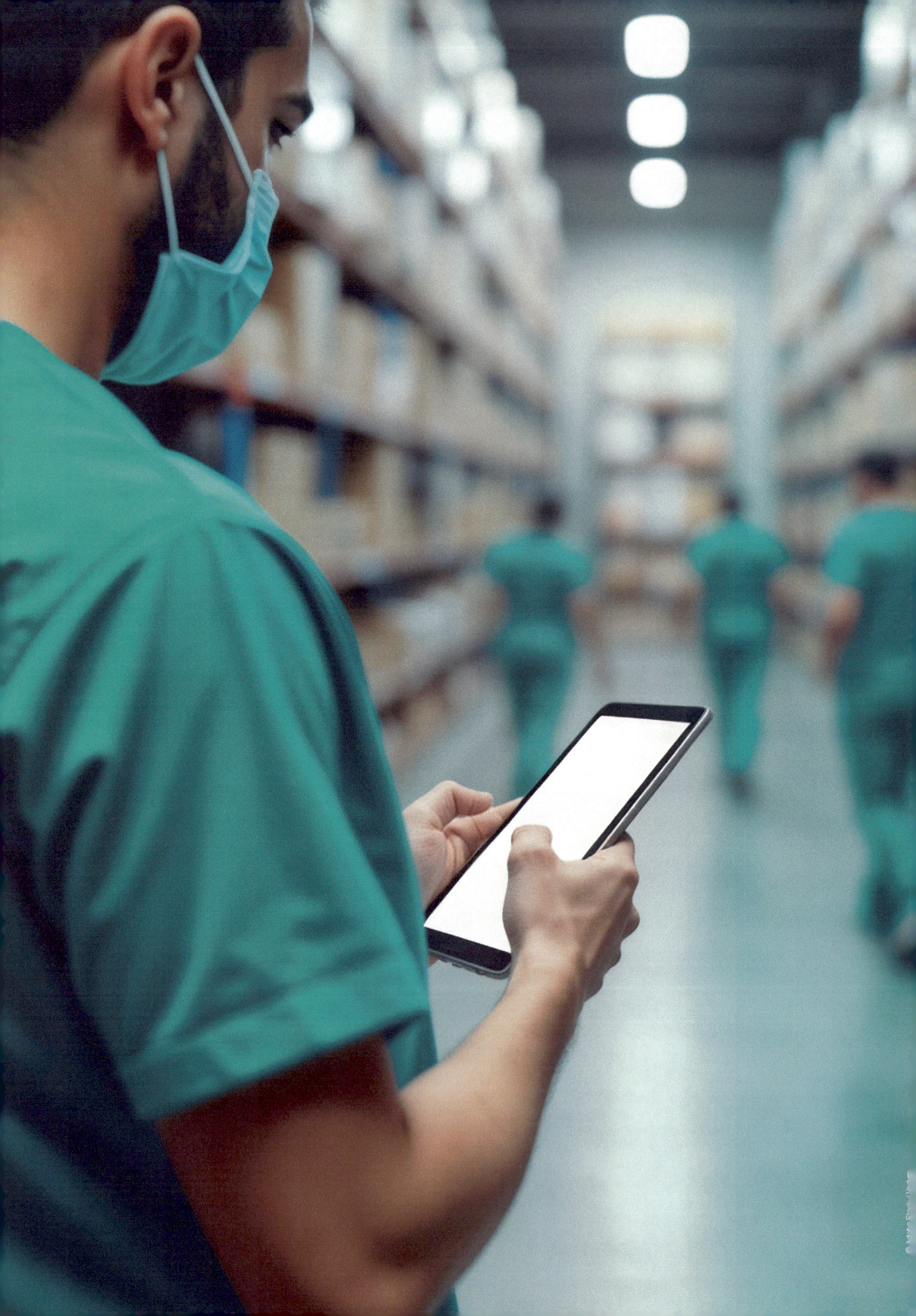

From NTMs data to trade impact analysis: A logical sequence

The TRAINS database enables transparency in how NTMs are used across countries, sectors and time. However, to use these complex data effectively for policy formulation and trade impact analysis, it is important to understand how to interpret them correctly and avoid common pitfalls.

A. Regulation level and measures level

Collecting NTMs data involves reviewing each regulation that can potentially affect exports or imports to identify all the measures it contains. Each identified measure is registered separately in the NTMs database. The database organizes information at two distinct levels: the regulation as issued by the country or economy (the legal document) and the measures (the specific requirements) within that regulation. Each regulation is thus associated with the list of measures it contains within the text. The details of the NTM data collection are explained in the NTMs data collection guidelines (UNCTAD, 2023).

The statistical analysis of NTMs is generally computed at the measure level, and not at the regulation level. Each NTM represents a single requirement in the text of the respective regulation. Thus, one regulation may contain multiple NTMs. Additionally, each NTM is associated to the list of products and trading partners that it applies to (see Figure 1).

Figure 1
One regulation can bear several NTMs

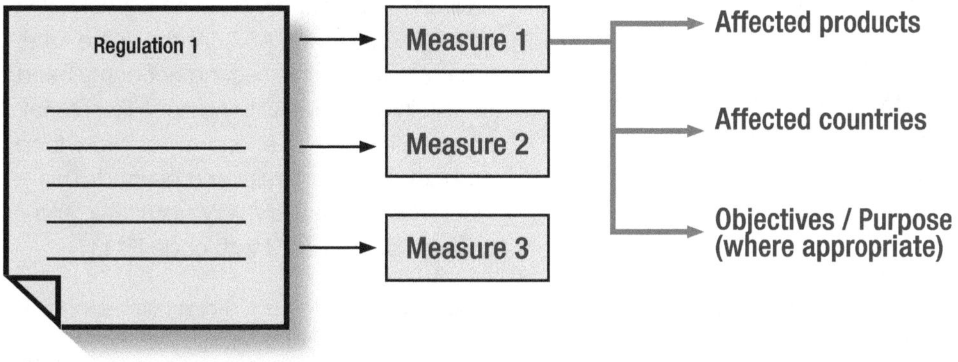

Comparing countries by the number of NTMs is misleading

Most of the meaningful statistical indicators assess trade implications from a product perspective. An assessment of the number of regulations would offer limited information.

To illustrate this point, it is useful to consider an example where a country implements a legal reform by combining several of the regulations into a single legal act, while at the same time not changing any of the content of the requirements on the products. Indeed, a country may have ten regulations on food products, each of them stating one different requirement. In contrast, another country may have only one legal act that contains those same ten NTMs. For companies trading those goods, it does not make any difference whether they must comply with one regulation or ten regulations, because in both countries they have to comply with the same ten product requirements, i.e., NTMs. Indeed, some legal texts are very broad in scope, while others are narrowly regulating.

Following this logic, comparing countries by the number of NTMs is misleading. The analysis needs to consider the number of products associated with that NTM requirement. For example, in a certain country there is a food act stating an inspection requirement –code A84– on edible fruit, which are all the products under 08 in the harmonized system (HS) classification; while in another country the food act requires an inspection – again code A84–, but this time applied to edible fruit and vegetables as well as meat and fish products. In this second case, the NTM with code A84 affects not only the chapter 08 on edible fruits, but also chapters 02, 03, 04, 05, and 07.[3, 4]

Study traded goods to have insight on NTMs' impact

The larger number of products affected by a single NTM may be reasonably estimated as an indicator of a larger impact, at least *a priori*. Of course, details of that measure, such as the stringency of the requirement and the enforcement level, could still be different and would determine the full cost of the measure to the traders. However, this is often beyond statistical analysis.[5]

This document, which focuses on statistical analysis of NTMs with the view of assessing the impact on trade, proposes indicators and methodology that are based on the unique combinations of:

- Reporter country or economy enforcing the NTMs,
- Partner country or economy being affected by the NTMs,
- Affected product at HS6 level,
- NTM code at the maximum level of disaggregation (6 digits), and
- Year of data collection.

The approach of this analysis makes use of the information that would list and describe all the requirements that fall on a single product, or group of products, of interest. As an example, edible fruits may need to go through an inspection (code A84), traceability requirements (code A85), plus tolerance limits for pesticide residues (code A21). In another economy, only the code that designate fresh fruits need to go through an inspection, but dry fruits have packaging requirements (code A33). At the same time, the importers in this second economy need to obtain a licence (with no specific criteria) from the ministry of economy for every food product, including fruits and beyond. This last NTM is potentially very restrictive, and it would be classified with code E111.

3 A chapter is a 2-digit number; a heading is a 4-digit number; a subheading is a 6-digit number in the HS nomenclature.

4 The NTM codes follow the international classification on NTMs: https://unctad.org/topic/trade-analysis/non-tariff-measures/NTM-classification

5 ESCAP and UNCTAD (2019) developed a statistical methodology that assesses NTMs well beyond the indicators presented here. It requires, however, additional details about the NTMs that are not contained in UNCTAD TRAINS.

Import measures and export measures are both issued in the same 'reporter' country or economy, and apply to imports and exports, respectively, of the same reporter. The former are import requirements which affect the imported products, while the latter are requirements for export. For example, a country may require that all exporters are registered before being allowed to export. This affects only export flows, and it is registered in the database under the P chapter of the NTMs classification. For a statistical analysis that matches NTMs with trade flows, the import measures, those under chapters A to O, are matched by reporter, partner and HS6 digit code with imports. The exports measures are matched with the export flows of that country. The NTM codes are described in the International Classification of NTMs.

B. Time dimension of the NTMs data in TRAINS

TRAINS database contains collected NTMs data from 2012 onwards. At the time, there were only a few economies in the database. Data collection progressed over the years. The annex shows the table of years and countries available. Data is available yearly only for some of the 'reporter' economies. For others, data collection was performed a few times, and for others, there is only one data point. This is for no other reason than the resources available to perform data collection.

Thus, the TRAINS database constitutes an unbalanced panel. This means that data are collected for different countries at different times. As such, each "data point" for a country or economy reflects the body of regulations in force at the time of data collection, regardless of the original date of enactment of each regulation. This is more comparable to a 'snapshot' of all NTMs in force at the time of collection, rather than a real-time update of newly enacted regulations.

It is important to emphasize that the TRAINS database does not record the legislative adoption date of individual NTMs as a primary indicator. Rather, when a country's data is surveyed, the dataset captures all regulations currently in effect at that point. Consequently, many regulations included in the database may have been adopted years — or even decades — earlier. The year of collection therefore reflects the timing of data availability, not the timing of regulatory creation. The date when a specific NTM came into force is, however, collected.

This structure can lead to common misinterpretations. For example, analysts may erroneously interpret the increase in the number of NTMs in the database over time as evidence of rising protectionism. This often reflects expanded economies' coverage in the database, not a proliferation of new regulations.

Careful interpretation of TRAINS data is essential for valid analysis. Misusing the time dimension or failing to account for the panel structure risks drawing incorrect conclusions about regulatory trends, trade restrictiveness, or policy evolution.

Some of the measures that were in force at the time of data collection may have been enacted several years before. Those will be included in the data set for that data point (a specific year and country when data is being collected), but not other measures that may have been enacted and repealed between two data collection points.

1. TRAINS online is an unbalanced panel dataset. One data point cannot be used as the sole information source for studying evolution of NTMs statistics over time.

Figure 2 depicts a typical situation in regulatory evolution in any country or economy.

Careful interpretation of TRAINS data is essential for valid analysis. Misusing the time dimension or failing to account for the panel structure risks drawing incorrect conclusions about regulatory trends, trade restrictiveness, or policy evolution.

Figure 2
Introduction of measures through time in any reporter

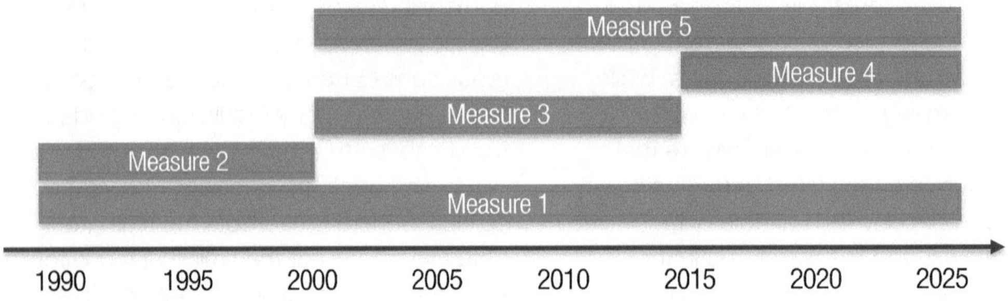

Source: UNCTAD, 2024.

- If data collection were performed in 1990, there would be measures 1 and 2 in the dataset because those were the only ones in force at that time.
- But if data collection is performed only in 2025, the dataset will include measures 1, 4 and 5 as those are the ones in force at the time. Measure 1 enacted in 1990 remains in force in 2025. Measures 4 and 5 were implemented after measure 1 but are also in force during the 2025 data collection. Note that measures 2 and 3 are not captured, as they are no longer in effect by that time. In this example, if we do not have data collection in 1990, or 2000, we would have only one data point for this country: 2025. Without continuous data collection, we would not know that measure 3 was in force from 2002 to 2015, or that measure 2 was in place from 1990 to 2000.

One data point cannot be used as the sole information source for studying the evolution of NTMs statistics over time.

One common misinterpretation is to take one recent data point for a reporter, in this case 2025, and observe the starting date for each of those regulations to infer the increase/decrease in the number of measures. As such, the misinterpretation of the data would conclude that this economy tripled its number of NTMs, as it had one measure in 1990 (measure 1) and three in 2025 (measures 1, 4 and 5).

If there had been continuous data collection since 1990, it would have been observed that this reporter had two measures from 1990 up to the year 2000 and then had three measures simultaneously in force from that time on. There has not been a change in the number of measures since the year 2000. Measures 2, 3 and 4 have been enacted to replace one another, only measure 5 is new. It is very common that countries and economies enact a new regulation in replacement of an old one. In this example, measure 3 replaces measure 2, and measure 4 replaces measure 3.

The measures in force at the time of data collection may have been enacted several years before. Those will be included in the data set for that data point (a specific year and country when data is being collected), but not other measures that may have been enacted and repealed before that date. In the case of the example, those are measures 2 and 3.

For this reason, it is methodologically incorrect to interpret the number of regulations recorded at the “start” of a collection year as representing new legislative activity. One data point cannot be used as the sole information source for studying the evolution of NTMs statistics over time.

2. How many more NTMs do we have now compared to one or two decades ago?

The UNCTAD TRAINS database on NTMs represents the most comprehensive and authoritative global repository of information on NTMs to date. As the database has grown over time, the number of countries and economies covered has increased from a small set of economies in 2012 to about 150 economies today. Only 17 economies are available in the database for the earliest year, 2012.[6]

Thus, there is certain analysis that can be misleading. It is for example not meaningful to compare the number of NTMs that the database contained in 2012 and the ones found today to derive conclusions about the variations in the total number of NTMs in the world. Because, of course, the total number of measures will be lower when there are only two economies in the database, compared to a recent year, when there are 150 economies (though with different years of data collection). Though in this case it is clear, there are other more subtle possible misunderstandings of the database structure that can lead to false conclusions.

If the analysis is made considering the data available year after year, it is then possible to compare the values for 2012 and today, especially using the indicators described in this document. For example, using the researcher file available for bulk download, it is possible to see that the share of imported products that face at least one measure in 2012 was around 60 per cent. When considering data for 2023, the value is 92 percent. Nevertheless, the increase may not be directly comparable either. The reason is that the researcher file presently has only 3 economies for the year 2023: Botswana, the European Union, and Vanuatu.[7] [8] Indeed, this same indicator is 72 percent for year 2022, when 24 economies are available. Consequently, the analysis year by year will be affected by the quantity of economies available, and probably also which ones, if there are significant differences in regulatory patterns by region or economic development.

While the database now includes about 150 economies, updates are irregular. Some have a few data points, when data has been updated a few times, while for other countries, data has only been collected once or twice throughout this period. Some of the most recent data is not yet included in the researcher file. For 2022, there are 24 economies available, though data collection was conducted in some more. The annex shows a table with the data availability that can also be found on the TRAINS website.

It is possible, however, to restrict the analysis to the economies for which data were available in two or more points in time. There are 50 economies in the data for which data has been collected at least twice, and 20 economies for which data has been collected seven times or more (see complete table for data availability in the annex).

As mentioned above, a yearly analysis of statistics could be misleading due to different economies being available. For a more representative analysis, it may be possible to split the panel data in two or three periods and take one observation by economy in each of those periods. The comparison would be made, then, for period 1, from 2012 to 2016, and then period 2, from 2017 to 2023.

6 In the researcher file, as of May 2025.

7 The European Union has many more imported products than the other two reporters, and so the European values may influence the total count of 'affected products'. The FI for European Union in 2012 was 94.7 percent, and it was 98.6 per cent in 2023, relatively stable. Botswana and Vanuatu recently graduated from LDC status, their FI was 63.4 per cent and 44 per cent, respectively in 2023. The LDC data available in 2012 are Afghanistan (FI 17.9 per cent), Burkina Faso (FI 15.1 per cent), and Nepal (FI 27.1 per cent). The FI corresponding to the lower income countries is typically lower than that of developed countries. If the European Union has considerably more imported product lines, the observations in the database outnumber the rest and influence the final value of 'global' FI.

8 More reporting economies are being regularly included in the researcher file, as they become available for the latest year. There are other reporters available for 2023, 2024 and forthcoming for 2025 by browsing in TRAINS online, but these have not yet been processed and included in the researcher file for bulk download at the time of writing.

Table 1
Evolution through time of coverage ratio for the economies available

Year	Coverage ratio	Number of economies available
2012	0.87	17
2013	0.89	14
2014	0.86	27
2015	0.79	49
2016	0.83	40
2017	0.82	31
2018	0.82	32
2019	0.87	26
2020	0.88	32
2021	0.92	13
2022	0.97	24
2023	0.97	3

Source: UNCTAD calculation based on TRAINS Online data.

Table 2 shows results using the year 2016 as cut date; period 1 is from 2012 to 2016, and period 2 from 2017 to 2023. The annex features a dumbbell bar which shows which economies are included in Period 1 and Period 2. There are 73 economies in period 1, from 2012 to 2016; and 88 economies in period 2, from 2017 to 2023. Out of these, 45 economies are present in both period 1 and 2 because data has been collected for those economies at least once in Period 1 and in Period 2, separately. The rest of the economies are only represented either in period 1 or 2 alternatively.

Figure 3 suggests that the values of indicators do not vary enormously, though in some cases it is noticeable. The large decrease for Eastern Africa could be linked to representativity of economies in the dataset. Globally, i.e. combining all economies, the value for coverage ratio is 0.79 for period 1 and 0.84 for period 2, but regional data suggest that some regions have varied more than others. Results suggest that developed countries had already high values and remained stable. The South and Central America had also relatively high values in period 2 but decreased slightly in period 2. Asian economies started from a lower level and clearly increased in between the two periods. African economies are largely being included in the TRAINS database during the second period only.

In the same way, the analysis by sector also suggests that the change in prevalence has increased over time in most cases, but moderately. It is also noticeable that values in some sectors are already high in period 1.

Table 2
Coverage ratio and prevalence score increase moderately between periods 1 and 2

There are 73 economies in period 1, from 2012 to 2016, and 88 economies in period 2, from 2017 to 2023

	Coverage ratio	Prevalence score
Period 1	0.794387817	3.164951086
Period 2	0.846446812	3.593472958

Source: UNCTAD calculation based on TRAINS Online data.

Figure 3

Values of coverage ratio and prevalence score vary moderately over time

Period 1, from 2012 to 2016, and Period 2, from 2017 to 2023

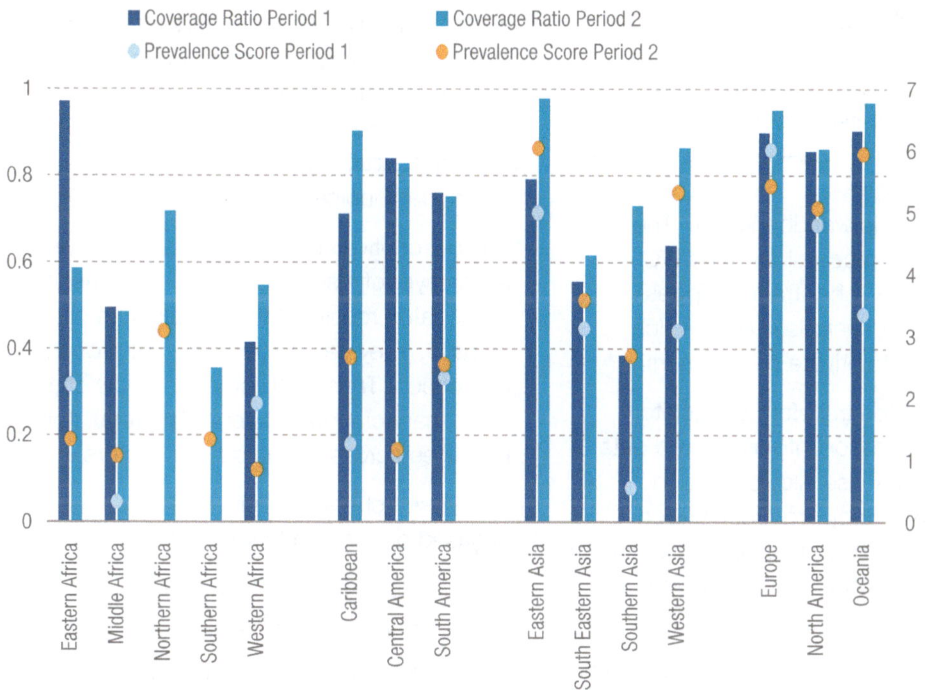

Source: UNCTAD calculation based on TRAINS Online data.
Note: Coverage ratio left scale, prevalence right scale.

Figure 4

Values of coverage ratio and prevalence score increased moderately over time

Period 1, from 2012 to 2016, and Period 2, from 2017 to 2023

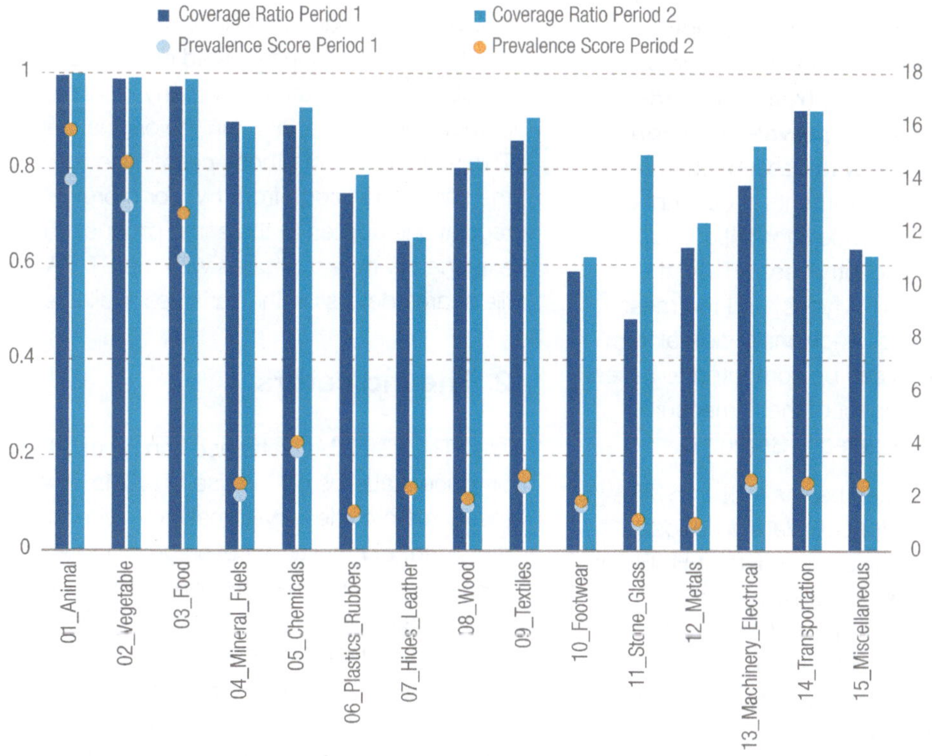

Source: UNCTAD calculation based on TRAINS Online data.
Note: Coverage ratio left scale, prevalence right scale.

C. NTMs' descriptive statistical indicators

1. Dataset for bulk download

The collected NTMs data is published through several dissemination tools, notably the UNCTAD TRAINS database accessible through trainsonline.unctad.org and WITS (wits.worldbank.org). The same data is also accessible in the ITC – UNCTAD - WTO Global Trade Helpdesk (https://globaltradehelpdesk.org), which is more catered to private sector users.

The data collection transforms regulatory text-based information into structured data. The TRAINS database allows users to organize the NTMs by product (HS code), type of measure (e.g., SPS, TBT), and country or economy of application (the reporter).

This data is published on the UNCTAD TRAINS website, which allows for browsing of the available NTMs data. The TRAINS NTMs database provides access to systematized information by product, measure type, countries, imposing and affected, and several other variables. It is therefore a valuable tool for using data for statistical analysis. The TRAINS NTMs database can be used directly to produce descriptive statistics, such as incidence measures. Three basic indicators: **frequency index, coverage ratio**, and **prevalence score**, are discussed below to describe the use of NTMs as policy instruments in descriptive statistics. They provide information, such as how often a country uses NTMs, the most common NTM types, and the most regulated sectors. Additionally, ad-valorem equivalent (AVE) can be computed to assess the economic impact of these measures. This is further explored in Section D.

Within the website, there is a file in STATA format available for bulk data download, which presents processed data at HS6 digit level for the latest available year in each country or economy (called the Researchers' file). The data in this file has undergone additional processing and cleaning to offer more consistency and suitability for statistical analysis. This data can be used to produce descriptive statistics, such as incidence measures, which can also be used as variables in more complex assessments such as gravity models. Details are described in the explanatory note downloadable from the TRAINS web page (https://api-trains2.unctad.org/get-researcher-file/3). From this structured database, a series of standard indicators can be derived.

The descriptive statistical indicators provide a first layer of insight. UNCTAD publishes the aggregated results of these indicators on its website. They can be freely used if properly referenced. These indicators are tools offering preliminary diagnostics regarding regulatory practices across countries and sectors.

The Researchers' file unit of analysis is based on the combination of:

1. Reporter country or economy enforcing the NTM,
2. Partner country or economy being affected by the NTM,
3. Affected product at HS6 level,
4. NTM code at the maximum level of disaggregation (6 digits), and
5. Year of data collection.

Elsewhere Researchers' file, each of these five-fold combinations is listed only once. The variable 'nbr' indicates how many identical combinations were found in the original data. This variable reflects those cases where the same NTM code from two (or more) regulations applies to the same product. The explanatory note that goes with the STATA file shares details on the variables available.

2. The indicators

The TRAINS NTMs database can be used to produce statistics on the use of NTMs. These measures provide a systematic overview of the extent of regulatory coverage within and across countries. They are used to analyze the regulatory landscape across countries, sectors, and time periods. The three most widely used indicators are frequency index, coverage ratio, and prevalence score, followed by ad-valorem equivalent (AVE).

A joint UNCTAD and World Bank publication (UNCTAD & World Bank, 2018) observed some stylized facts. For example, developed countries tend to have deeper levels of regulation, covering more sectors and with a higher number of NTMs. The objective may be to ensure consumer safety or product quality, among others. Chapters A and B, in the NTMs classification, which cover SPS and TBT measures, are used more frequently by developed countries. Less developed countries have significantly fewer regulations in these areas, on average, indicating that some sectors might not be well regulated.

As well as revealing the policy tools in place by economy, the data reveal which sectors are more or less regulated, and with which type of policy tool. For example, the data for the year 2022 shows that countries had, on average, about 10 measures on each agricultural product. Some countries are imposing 20 measures or more, on average, on each agri-food product. See Table 3. Trading companies need to comply to all of those for accessing that market. It is also relevant for businesses to understand what type of measures those are.

A comparison of policy tools between countries is particularly useful when considering regional integration or market access issues, as major regulatory differences between trading partners add difficulties for traders particularly in small and medium size enterprises that relatively more often trade regionally rather than globally. TRAINS offers granular information that is very valuable to analyse if the measures applied to the own economy are similar/dissimilar to the ones applied in the market to be accessed. Research suggests that it may be more costly for companies to adapt to a regulatory scheme that is very different to one already applied internally.[9]

Finally, data may be used to test hypotheses in economic models and to indicate the possible impact of NTMs on trade.

Table 3
Prevalence score in agri-food sector for the countries/economies available for the year 2022

Economy	Prevalence score
AUS	20.1
CAN	12.1
COD	6.5
COG	1.9
COM	4.5
EUN	19.1
FJI	11.4
GAB	5.7
GMB	11.7
JPN	9.7
LSO	0.5
MMR	20.2
NAM	7.6
PNG	13.3
RWA	13.5
SLB	11.7
SWZ	3.2
SYC	4.3
TGO	7.2
TZA	12.1
UGA	3.0
VNM	22.6
VUT	13.9
ZMB	1.9

Source: UNCTAD calculation based on TRAINS Online data.

The "frequency index" and "coverage ratio" are the two basic indicators used to measure the pervasiveness of NTMs in an economy. Both rely on variables that reflect whether a measure is applied to a specific product. A third indicator, the "prevalence score" (also known as the Intensity Index) captures the extent to which a specific type of NTM is used. It measures the number of distinct NTMs for a given product, the average number across a group of products, or the average number for a given country or economy. These indicators are fully explained in the subsections below.

9 UNCTAD developed an approach to measure regulatory similarity in regions including relative to international standards. See https://unctad.org/topic/trade-analysis/non-tariff-measures/NTMs-policy-support/regional-integration for the approach and several applications.

While these metrics illustrate the incidence and variety of NTMs used as policy tools, they do not capture their economic impact. They do not reveal the costs to exporters and importers, nor if they restrict or enhance trade, or to what extent. In some cases, NTMs could facilitate trade, especially when requirements are already met or when they build consumer trust in imports. To assess this impact of NTMs on trade, AVEs offers more insight.

a. Further technical notes to the computation

Partial coverage. Following various UNCTAD publications, partial coverage is not used in the computation of the indicators. More information can be seen in the explanatory note that can be downloaded with the bulk data set in TRAINS as well as in UNCTAD (2024).

The main reason lies in the level of data collection across countries. In some cases, data is collected at the tariff-line level (8 digits or more), while in others, it is only available at the 6-digit level.

For the reporters that have products classified at 8 digits or more, partial coverage is used when only certain tariff-line items within a 6-digit code are (fully) affected by an NTM. This results in a "partial coverage" indication at the 6-digit level. However, for countries where data is collected solely at the 6-digit level, it is not possible to distinguish between actual partial coverage (as defined in the legislation and outlined in the Guidelines for Data Collection) and cases where only some tariff-line items are affected. This limitation can lead to ambiguity in interpreting the extent of NTMs coverage.

When the analysis includes NTMs with partial coverage indication, the indicator values clearly increase.

Bilateral dimension. Some NTMs implemented by countries target specific trading partners rather than applying universally. This often reflects differences in legislative approaches. While some countries/economies explicitly specify requirements or exceptions of requirements for certain trade partners in their legislation, others primarily adopt unilateral measures that apply to products regardless of origin.

This bilateral dimension of the data is considered in the computation of indicators. For example, in calculating the frequency index, the numerator includes all product–partner combinations affected by one or more NTMs. The denominator consists of all possible combinations of products at the HS 6-digit level and all trading partners. This approach ensures that the index reflects the selective application of NTMs across different bilateral relationships without dropping this information from the analysis.

b. The frequency index

The frequency index (FI) measures the share of product lines affected by at least one NTM. It provides a sense of how widespread regulatory measures are across an economy's import or export structure.

The formula is the following:

$$F_{it} = \frac{\sum D_{ijpt}\, M_{ijpt}}{\sum M_{ijpt}} . 100$$

The FI is a ratio calculated using two dummy variables in the numerator (sums are over *j* and *p*):

A. D_{ijpt}, the presence (or absence) of at least one NTM on product *p* (HS6 digit level).

B. M_{ijpt}, which equals 1 for every product imported by this reporting country or economy.

- Subindex *i* and *j* represent reporter and partner economies.

The indicator F_{it} is computed for economy *i* at time *t*, *i.e.*, using the data for a certain point in time. The sum in the numerator is the total number of "affected" products, and the denominator is the sum of all products; the FI is the ratio between them.

There are alternatives to the set products considered in the computation. The denominator may be computed as:

a. The total existing number of products. If calculated at HS6, there are around 5200 products. In this case the M_{ijpt} is about 5200

b. Only the traded lines, i.e. the count of product items. The M_{ijpt} are only the ones that are imported (or exported) and excluding those that have zero trade value.

- For example, if a country imports only 2000 products, and has NTMs on 1000 of those products, the FI will be:
  a) Close to 20 per cent if using the total universe of products (∑_p=5200).
  b) 50 per cent if calculated using only traded products (∑_p=2000).

C. The usual criteria adopted by UNCTAD for the computation is to use only the traded lines in the denominator, i.e., only those products that are imported (exported), leaving aside those products that may or may not be affected by an NTM but that are not traded (option b).

As a share, the value of FI is between 0 and 100. It can be computed at the country level, over a group of countries at the regional level, or on a subgroup of products, e.g., agricultural products or industrial products.

UNCTAD also publishes the computed results for the indicators by chapter of the NTMs classification. i.e., the frequency index of SPS is the share of products that are affected by at least one SPS measure. The same can be done for the rest of the chapters, TBT, finance measures, or export measures, for example.

The analysis can compare how a country or economy's value evolves over time, by using two or more data points, provided that data has been collected multiple times in that economy. This is possible because data has been collected using the same methodology every time.

To calculate the FI for import-related measures, NTMs from Chapters A to O are matched against the list of imported products. For the export FI, which corresponds to Chapter P, the relevant export NTMs are matched with the list of exported products. This ensures that the FI accurately reflects the presence of NTMs in relation to the direction of trade—import or export data must be used.

c. The coverage ratio

The second measure, the coverage ratio (CR), is the share of trade subject to NTMs. It adjusts the frequency index by weighing it according to the value of trade that is affected. It shows what share of total import (or export) value is subject to at least one NTM. Similarly to the frequency index, it can also be computed for a country, or for a region, or a group of products.

The coverage ratio is calculated using the following formula:

$$C_{it} = \frac{\sum D_{ijpt} \, V_{ijpt}}{\sum V_{ijpt}} .100$$

Where (sums are over *j* and *p*):

D. D_{ijpt} is a dummy variable that equals 1 if an NTM is applied to product *p* (HS 6-digit level) by reporting country *i* and partner *j* at time *t*, and 0 otherwise.

E. V_{ijpt} represents the trade value (imports or exports) of product *p* between reporting country *i* and partner *j* at time *t*.

The numerator captures the sum of the import (export) value of those traded products that are affected by an import (export) NTM at time *t*. It is then divided by the total value of imports (exports), for the country *i* and a partner *j* at time *t*.

Usually, the CR is computed using the average trade value for the last three years (bilateral and by HS6), so that there would be less zero trade values.

When the analysis is done by chapter of the NTMs classification, it is possible to calculate the share of trade that is affected by, for example, at least one TBT measure.

To calculate the CR for import-related measures, NTMs from chapters A to O are matched with the list of imported products, along with their corresponding trade values. For the export coverage ratio, which pertains to chapter P, export NTMs are matched with the list of exported products and their trade values. This allows the CR to reflect the share of trade (by value) that is subject to one or more NTMs, providing a weighted measure of regulatory impact on trade flows.

d. Prevalence score

The prevalence score (PS) measures the average number of measures applied to a given product group. It can be used, for example, to assess what group of products is affected by the largest number of NTMs on average. For instance, it can be computed to see if agricultural products are affected by more measures, compared to industrial products, or to compare the average number of measures for a specific product group among different countries.

The formula is similar to the previous cases:

$$P_{it} = \frac{\sum \mathrm{D_{ijpt}} N_{\mathrm{ijpt}}}{\sum \mathrm{M_{ijpt}}}$$

Where (sums are over *j* and *p*):

F. D_{ijpt}, the presence (or absence) of an NTM on the product ***p*** at the HS6 digit level.

G. N_{ijpt} is the number of NTMs on product ***p***.

H. M_{ijpt} is the total number of products (those with and without NTMs).

Similarly to the previous indicators, the set of products used in the calculation can be restricted to traded products only (i.e., imported products for import measures or exported products for export measures), or it can include the entire universe of products at the HS 6-digit level or the selected product group.

Inclusion of zeroes in the average. The average includes zero values for products not affected by any NTM. The advantage of including the zeroes in the average is that it reflects the average regulatory burden across all products, not just those subject to NTMs. It is analogous to how average tariffs are calculated. When calculating the average tariff for a country or sector, normally all zero tariffs are also included in the calculation. It is advisable to do the same for the number of NTMs.

However, including zeroes also means that the FI (the share of products affected by at least one NTM) will influence the prevalence score. A low frequency index will naturally lower the average number of NTMs per product. If the goal is to analyze the intensity of NTM application—that is, how many NTMs are applied when they are present—it may be more appropriate to exclude zeroes from the average.

Chapter-level analysis. When presenting PS by NTM chapter (e.g., SPS or TBT measures), it is generally preferable not to include zeroes. This is because the number of products affected by a specific type of NTM (such as SPS) may be small relative to the total number of traded products. Including all unaffected products would dilute the average, potentially underrepresenting the actual regulatory intensity within that chapter. If the number of products affected by an SPS within the set of all imported products is small, then the average number of NTMs will be small. This is not because there are few SPS measures being applied, but because the number of products not having SPS measures is very large, and there are a lot of zeroes.

Purpose of the prevalence score. The PS captures the regulatory intensity by counting how many NTMs apply simultaneously to a single product. This helps identify cases where multiple NTMs may compound compliance complexity, signaling potentially higher regulatory burden for those products.

3. The uses of indicators

The inventory measures are descriptive indicators and can be used as a first layer of analysis in the analysis of NTMs. This offers essential insights into the regulatory environment that shapes international trade. Although inherently descriptive, these indicators are valuable for understanding how regulations are distributed across economies, sectors, and time. They do not, by themselves, provide estimates of trade costs or economic impact. However, their analytical value lies in its simplicity, bringing overall insight on the body of legal and technical regulations that affect trade.

Transparency. At the most basic level, NTMs indicators provide transparency. They allow researchers and policymakers to visualize and quantify the presence of NTMs across different countries or groups of products. For instance, by calculating how many product lines are subject to at least one NTM, the frequency index is a first assessment of the economy's regulatory practice, through statistical incidence of NTMs. When further analysis takes into account the type of measure by chapter of the NTMs classification, it is possible to assess the choice that the economy makes to use certain types of measures more. Those countries that use fewer technical measures, for example, are probably those that have less technical capacity to develop the standards and this normally goes in line with the sophistication of their metrology systems[10] and quality infrastructure. These countries may rely more on quantitative regulatory instruments such as quotas or non-technical licences.

NTMs indicators also act as a proxy for the regulatory complexity within a country's trading system. Countries with many NTMs, or with regulations spread across many product lines, may face greater compliance burdens for exporters and importers. In this way, the number of NTMs recorded can be used as a measure of the regulatory complexity facing traders, even if it does not quantify the actual cost burden. Indeed, this information may feed into econometric models to assess impact on trade, such as gravity analysis.[11] They are also used in the computation of AVEs.

Cross-country comparisons and benchmarking. Beyond enhancing transparency, NTMs indicators serve as powerful tools for comparative analysis. They enable benchmarking across countries or regions, helping to assess whether a country or economy's regulatory intensity aligns with global norms or deviates significantly. Such deviations may indicate either excessive restrictiveness or insufficient regulation. These insights can support trade negotiations, regional integration initiatives, and national policy evaluations.

For such comparisons to be most meaningful, it is recommended that analysis is carried out at the product level, and not the regulation level, as described above. Analyzing the share of affected products (frequency index), particularly when combined with trade values (coverage ratio) and the average number of NTM applied per product (prevalence score), allows for a more detailed understanding of how regulatory measures are distributed across sectors and trading partners.

If, alternatively, the analysis only compares the number of legal texts issued by government agencies, it loses much of its economic value. This is because such counts do not capture the depth or scope of specific requirements embedded within those legal instruments.

Targeting areas for further analysis. Another vital use of NTMs indicators is in identifying patterns and priorities for deeper investigation. Since the indicators map NTMs by type, sector, and product, they can spotlight areas where regulatory activity is unusually scarce, dense or growing. This helps researchers and regulators focus their attention on high-impact sectors such as agriculture, pharmaceuticals, or electronics—areas where NTMs are frequently used and may have significant implications for both public policy objectives and market access. Moreover, a high prevalence score may indicate areas that are more heavily regulated. By studying the

10 Metrology is the scientific approach of measuring, e.g., residue limits of pesticides in food.

11 Gravity analysis is a widely used empirical framework used in international trade studies that explains bilateral trade flows by relating them to economic size, distance, and other trade cost variables. Developed and codified in UNCTAD and WTO (2016).

number (and type) of measures enforced on these sectors, the country or economy may assess the combined impact of potential multiple regulatory ministries or departments. Such insights are crucial for trade facilitation initiatives, where reducing unnecessary or overlapping regulations can deliver meaningful improvements in efficiency and competitiveness, lowering trade costs.

Monitoring regulatory trends over time. NTMs indicators also provide a useful tool for monitoring regulatory trends over time when they are computed, taking into account the panel data dimension, i.e. using the years when data has been actually collected for that economy. Analysts can use frequency and coverage variations over those selected years to assess how regulatory practices evolve. This temporal dimension is key for understanding the dynamics of trade regulation—whether countries are implementing reforms, increasing the scope of NTMs in terms of coverage, increasing reliance on certain types of NTMs, or even moving toward greater regulatory harmonization with trade partners.

In sum, the analysis of NTMs indicators is foundational to the examination of regulatory measures in trade. It offers clarity, structure, and direction in a field where policy is inherently complex and fragmented. While these indicators must be interpreted considering their limitations (see subsection below), they are essential instruments for making NTMs visible, comparable, and actionable within the broader framework of trade policy analysis.

Indeed, the indicators are a first step in profiling the practices for NTMs use that can shed light on areas which could be considered by policymakers to use trade as an engine for growth, competitiveness and development. They serve as a starting point for further, deeper analyses, which can explore the trade impact and economic consequences of these measures in more detail.

Correlation with NTM variables. It is also possible to compare the presence or absence of NTMs on products to the level of tariffs for those same products. UNCTAD (2018) shows that there is a negative correlation between the two, especially with the prevalence score. Products that have a higher number of NTMs tend to have lower levels of tariffs.

In a similar way, NTMs can be matched to variables, such as gross domestic product per capita. Usually, countries with higher level of income have more NTMs in place.

4. Limitations of NTMs indicators

NTMs indicators, by their nature, do not directly measure the cost or impact of NTMs on trade, development, market access, or welfare. They provide descriptive information about the presence, scope, and breadth of regulations in force at a particular point in time. While they are an essential starting point for understanding the regulatory landscape, they do not offer a direct measure of how costly or restrictive those measures are in economic terms.

The indicators primarily reflect the number of legal requirements. They do not capture the stringency of the requirements contained within those legal texts. As such, while NTMs indicators are useful for identifying patterns and outliers, they are to be complemented by qualitative assessments of regulatory content, or other quantitative assessments, such as AVEs.

Descriptive statistical indicators do not reflect policy intent either. An economy with a high number of recorded NTMs may be engaged in legitimate public policy objectives — such as ensuring food safety, environmental protection, or consumer rights — rather than protectionist behaviour.

They also do not measure the welfare effects. Indicators can show where regulations are, but they do not assess whether those regulations are ultimately beneficial or harmful to consumers, producers, or the economy as a whole. In the same way that the presence of an NTM does not necessarily constitute a barrier to trade, their existence does not imply either that the regulation is well designed or achieves the public policy objective.

Furthermore, the criteria used for computing the indicators may also pose limitations. For example, if the frequency index uses the traded products only for its computation, and not the universe of products, it may hide regulations affecting some of the non-traded products. Those NTMs could potentially be so restrictive as to preclude trade.

Moving beyond inventories may require the application of econometric analysis. Researchers and policymakers can select, for example, specific sectors, countries, or measure types for further investigation, guided by the patterns observed in the descriptive analysis. Econometric models, such as gravity models adapted for NTMs, allow for the empirical estimation of how NTMs affect trade flows (see section D).

5. Selected indicator results

This section shows an application for the indicators. Figure 5 shows the results of the coverage ratio and prevalence score computed over the full list of countries contained in the TRAINS database, using the latest available data point, i.e., the latest year of data collection for each economy (see annex for full table of data availability).

The results show that the three sectors with higher values for both indicators are agricultural products, animal products, and food products. Across these three sectors, almost every HS 6-digit product for each reporter–partner pair is affected by at least one NTM. This is illustrated by the bars that are close to 1 for these three sectors in the figure.

The dataset can contain up to 1.3 million observations, calculated as the product of approximately 130 reporters (counting the European Union as one economy), around 100 agricultural products in their

Figure 5

High values of coverage ratio and prevalence score for agri-food sectors

Global values for latest year of data collection of all countries in TRAINS combined

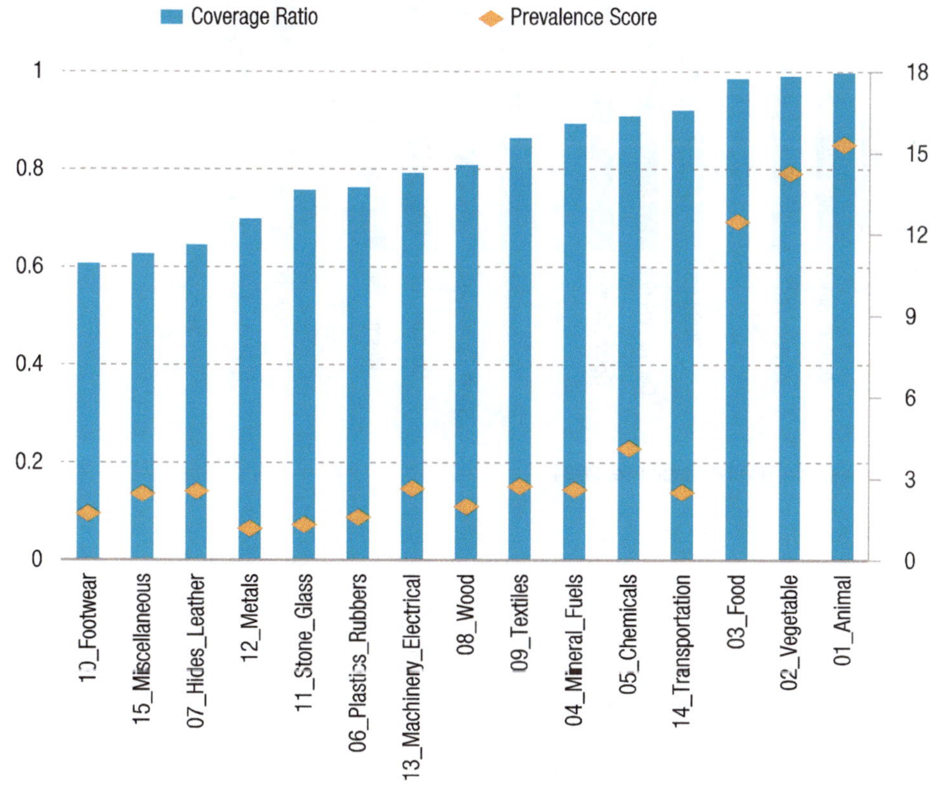

Source: UNCTAD based on TRAINS database, 2024.
Note: Coverage ratio left axis and prevalence score right axis.

import baskets, and roughly 100 trading partners. The vast majority of these observations involve at least one NTM.

The prevalence score is also the highest for these three sectors. Each product in these sectors bear between 12 and 15 NTMs on average. It is represented by the dots, that corresponds to the right axis in the figure.

The sectors with lower incidence are footwear, miscellaneous manufacturers, and leather products, while those with lower number of NTMs (prevalence score) are metals and stone and glass.

Figure 6 shows the same information computed over regions. There is much variation within and across regions, but African countries tend to have lower shares of its imports affected by NTMs, compared to American and Asian countries, and especially Europe, North America and Oceania.

The prevalence score is also higher for these latter 3 country groupings. African countries, together with Central American and Caribbean countries exhibit lower prevalence scores.

Figure 6

Coverage ratio and prevalence score by region

Global values for latest year of data collection of all countries in TRAINS combined

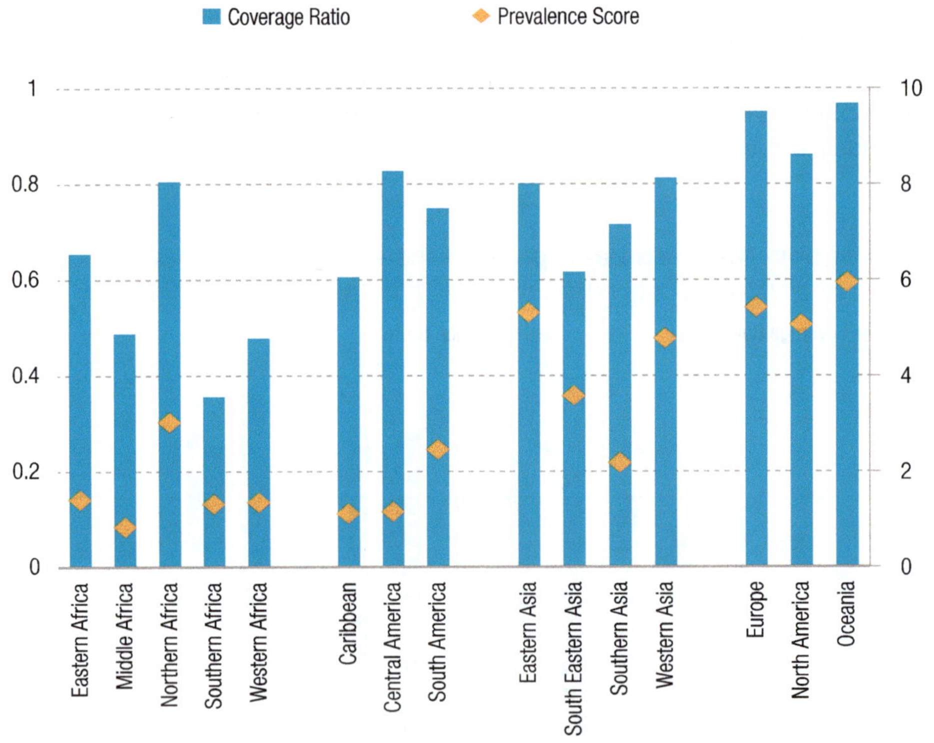

Source: UNCTAD based on TRAINS database, 2024.

D. Complementing NTMs indicators: Econometric techniques and AVEs

1. Moving toward quantification

While inventory indicators such as the frequency index and coverage ratio provide a transparent view of the regulatory landscape, they remain fundamentally descriptive. They indicate where regulations are present and how extensively they apply, but they stop short of explaining how these regulations affect trade flows, prices, or welfare. Quantitative impact assessment may be necessary to support meaningful trade and regulatory policy decisions.

Gravity models are the most widely used tools to estimate the impact of NTMs on trade outcomes. These are used in the estimation of ad valorem equivalents (AVEs), which express the estimated impact of NTMs as if they were tariffs—i.e., as a percentage increase in the price of a product due to the regulation/s applied to it. This translation into a tariff-equivalent form enables direct comparison between NTMs and traditional trade policy instruments. It also gives policymakers a clearer sense of the magnitude of regulatory barriers. Furthermore, to assess the impact of NTMs on economies with partial or general equilibrium models, AVEs are necessary.

2. Ad Valorem Equivalents (AVEs) of NTMs

The AVEs of NTMs provides an estimate of the average additional trade costs due to the presence of NTMs. UNCTAD website publishes the computed values for AVEs at the bilateral economy level at the Global Trade Analysis Project (GTAP) sector level.[12]

The estimation of AVEs is the most widely accepted method for translating the trade impact of NTMs into a format that is directly comparable to tariffs. By expressing the effects of regulations as a percentage of product value, AVEs allow researchers and policymakers to evaluate how restrictive NTMs are—enabling comparisons across sectors, products, countries, and types of trade policy instruments.

The database provided by UNCTAD for AVEs of "border NTMs"[13] estimates this indicator based on compliance costs associated with NTMs imposed at borders, such as customs regulations, licensing, inspections, and traceability. It includes only those technical measures that are border measures. These AVEs represent the additional costs NTMs impose on imports, expressed as the equivalent uniform tariff that would have the same trade impact. The data is consistent with the GTAP version 11 database and uses UNCTAD TRAINS NTMs data.

These AVEs can be used directly as shocks to the GTAP model. The dataset includes 162,760 observations, covering 85 importing countries (plus the European Union and residual regions) and 99 exporting countries (plus the European Union and residual regions). AVEs are calculated at the 6-digit HS classification level and aggregated to the GTAP level using trade weights based on 2017 import flows (the base year for GTAP 11). The database provides trade-weighted and simple averages of AVEs by region, sector, and bilateral trade relationships.

[12] https://unctad.org/topic/trade-analysis/data-statistics-and-trends. GTAP is a widely used and accepted general equilibrium model and network (www.gtap.org).

[13] Border NTMs refer to NTMs that are applied at the point of entry or exit of goods and are directly related to import/export procedures, controls, or requirements. NTMs applied at the border (border NTMs), include custom controls, quota licensing, pre-shipment inspections, additional fees paid at customs, among many others. Border measures include many categories under different chapters of the classification. In detail, they include the codes: A14, A140, A15, A150, A81, A810, A84, A840, A85, A850, A851, A852, A853, A859, A86, A860, A89, A890, B14, B140, B15, B150, B81, B810, B84, B840, B85, B850, B851, B852, B853, B859, B89, B890, C00, C000, C10, C100, C20, C200, C30, C300, C40, C400, C90, C900, E10, E100, E11, E110, E111, E112, E113, E119, E12, E120, E121, E122, E129, F40, F400, F60, F600, F61, F610, F62, F620, F63, F630, F64, F640, F65, F650, F67, F670, F80, and F800.

The estimation methodology follows Kee and Nicita (2022), using econometric models to isolate the effects of NTMs on trade quantities. The AVEs are constructed as the proportionate change in quantity imported due to NTMs, divided by the aggregated price elasticity of demand. The paper from Kee and Nicita (2022) also includes technical details, country and product coverage, and references for further information.

UNCTAD also provides AVEs for both technical (chapters A and B for SPS and TBT) and non-technical measures (other chapters referring to import NTMs), following the international classification of NTMs. This dataset is consistent with the GTAP version 10 database and uses UNCTAD TRAINS NTMs data as the basis for the calculation.

Computed AVEs by UNCTAD are available from the website.[14]

a. Stylized facts

According to Nicita and Koloskova (2025), the costs related to border NTMs, i.e., border AVEs, vary significantly between countries and across sectors. In terms of sectors, natural resource commodities usually incur lower border NTMs costs. In contrast, many agricultural commodities face higher border costs because of heightened concerns about quality and safety. The AVEs of manufactured goods are generally between those of agricultural products and those of natural resources. Among manufactured goods, textiles and apparel have relatively low AVEs, while the vehicle transportation sector has the highest AVEs.

AVEs also vary across geographic regions. Overall, the costs associated with border NTMs are lower for imports into South Asia and Western Europe, while they are relatively higher for imports into East Asia, Latin America, the Middle East and North Africa.

From the perspective of exporters, the AVEs imposed by the importing country show an even greater variance across regions. Exporters from different regions often face varying AVEs in their destination markets, due to both the composition of their export baskets and the presence of bilateral NTMs. This is the result combining the cost of market access and the cost of each exporter region's conditions.

Notably, costs related to border NTMs are not generally lower for intra-regional trade, except for trade within Europe and within North America, largely due to the presence of regional trade agreements facilitating border crossing.

Border NTMs are those that are closely linked to traditional trade facilitation measures being implemented at customs. Thus, this set of AVEs focuses on quantifying the effect of only those types of measures. For an assessment of the technical measures such as SPS or TBT, users can refer to the dataset on technical and non-technical AVEs.

Nicita and Koloskova (2025) simulate an exercise that illustrates the impact of reducing border NTMs costs on trade flows and other economic indicators. This approach allows for an assessment of the overall importance of border-related costs in affecting global trade patterns, delving into the effects on trade between regions and sectoral trade. Specifically, the model will help to identify which sectors and regions stand to benefit the most from such reductions.

In general, the costs associated with border NTMs tend to be lower for transactions occurring under Regional Trade Agreements (RTAs). This is not surprising, as many RTAs have specific provisions aimed at streamlining customs procedures and trade facilitation mechanisms for reducing

[14] Data download for: AVEs of border measures. Available for Version 11, Version 10 , Version 9. AVEs for technical and non-technical measures. Available for Version 10, Version 9. Available at: https://unctad.org/topic/trade-analysis/data-statistics-and-trends
Note for the use of the database on AVE of NTM available at:
https://unctad.org/system/files/information-document/AVE_GTAP_README_rev1.pdf

cross-border transaction costs. Indeed, recent deep regional trade agreement negotiations have been largely focused on harmonizing, simplifying, or mutually recognizing non-tariff measures. Cadot et al. (2015) show that the average regional trade agreement cuts the distance in regulatory structure significantly by about 40 per cent. This analysis does not only include border measures but also behind the border technical measures. Moreover, UNCTAD (2024) shows that potential welfare gains from the implementation of the African Continental Free Trade Agreement is more than twice as high when technical measures converge, compared to where only non-technical measures, i.e., often called non-tariff barriers, are addressed. Potential gains are more than four times higher if instead of converging to regional standards, technical standards converge to international standards.

This type of analysis is only possible after the computation of the AVEs, as these represent a quantifiable cost impact measure and can be used as an input in this type of general equilibrium analysis.

b. Methodology for AVEs in a nutshell

Estimating AVEs is key to quantifying the impact on trade and thus to inferring the consequences if the NTMs policy pattern varies. However, this is methodologically challenging. Kee and Nicita (2022) provide an estimation based on a gravity model of trade. The results showed that AVEs can range from 5 to 20 per cent, with high values found in sectors like food, or agriculture.[15]

c. The uses and limitations of AVEs

By quantifying the trade restrictiveness of NTMs, AVEs help identify sectors where regulatory measures may be unnecessarily burdensome. This information can guide efforts to streamline regulations, negotiate trade agreements, and implement trade facilitation measures. Furthermore, understanding the AVEs of NTMs provides valuable insights for policy makers, and enables them to balance trade objectives with legitimate regulatory goals, such as protecting health and the environment. Very costly NTMs may be needed for important policy objectives.

The AVE analysis in Kee and Nicita (2022) assessed all the NTMs affecting a product and does not isolate a particular NTM or a particular type of NTM. The analysis uses absence or presence of NTMs on a certain product, regardless of the number or the type of measures. The analysis is, thus, not able to distinguish which of the NTMs is the more restrictive, when there is more than one on a certain product.[16]

Furthermore, though the approach to estimate AVEs that has been elaborated here is clear and widely referenced, it remains a research area. The AVE values, thus, may vary according to the methodology employed in the computation.

Moreover, in the same way as high values of the incidence indicators do not necessarily indicate that the NTMs are barriers or have protectionist intent, the same applies to high AVE values. Many NTMs are instituted to serve essential policy objectives, such

[15] The Kee and Nicita (2022) AVE analysis provides an estimation based on a gravity model with the following characteristics: a) The dependent variable is the log of expected import quantity. The explanatory variables include not only NTM incidence (presence or absence of an NTM), but also tariffs, market power interaction terms (shares of trade flows) and other gravity variables. b) The model estimates the semi-elasticity of trade with respect to tariffs and NTMs. c) The coefficients for tariffs and NTMs vary bilaterally following the assumed effect of importers' and exporters' market power. The bilateral trade shares used are: the exporter's absolute market power, the exporter's relative market power in the importer's market, and the importer's market power.

The AVE of an NTM is computed by estimating first the proportionate change in quantity imported due to the presence of the NTM, and then using the elasticity of trade with respect to a one percentage point increase in the tariff to convert the proportionate change in quantity imported due to the NTM in terms of ad valorem equivalents. More details can be found in Kee and Nicita (2022).

[16] Cadot et al. (2015) use a different approach and distinguish SPS, TBT and other NTMs (called NTBs in that paper). The AVEs show that the technical measures account in most regions for the highest trade costs stemming from NTMs.

as protecting public health, ensuring environmental sustainability, or maintaining food safety standards, especially technical NTMs. Regulatory measures designed to prevent market failures or protect consumers may impose significant compliance costs, but their broader societal benefits often justify these burdens. Therefore, policymakers should avoid interpreting high AVEs automatically as indicators of problematic or illegitimate regulation. Rather, AVEs should serve as initial signals to identify regulatory measures that warrant closer examination, distinguishing between justified and disproportionate restrictions through comprehensive legal and economic assessments.

To address this limitation, the border AVEs have been computed. For the border AVEs only the NTM codes that represent border measures and which can be associated with direct burdensome compliance at the border have been selected. These are usually the direct costs that are targeted for reduction in regional trade agreements and the WTO Trade Facilitation Agreement.

Chapter III

Conclusion: Combining descriptive and impact analysis

Conclusion: Combining descriptive and impact analysis

NTMs have a large impact on trade costs and due to their bilaterally divergent de facto impact on market access conditions, they have no most-favored nation nature but often disproportionately negatively affect smaller enterprises, vulnerable groups and poorer economies (UNCTAD, 2022). Understanding the role of NTMs in shaping international trade and development requires systematic analysis. This in turn requires data availability, where tremendous progress has been made in one decade, and understanding how to access the data. The latter is explained in "Making sense of non-tariff measures: A user's guide to accessing and analysing the data**", UNCTAD (2024a).**

This handbook presents possible analytical approaches that are useful to understand the universe of NTMs and their impact on trade and development in order to support policymakers to achieve public policy objectives, including designing regulations with minimal costs while maintaining essential objectives. The handbook also discusses analytical constraints due to data and index limitations.

Common misleading analysis that is addressed in this report includes counting regulations to infer the depth of regulatory policies affecting trade, or even counting the NTMs in force in a certain economy. Instead of noting how many legal texts, or how many NTMs an economy may have, assessing the share of the number of goods or trade that is affected by NTMs is more insightful. TRAINS database offers granular data that allows this type of analysis. Another common error is to infer the evolution (typically growth) of NTMs by using just one data point of the data collection. TRAINS database is an unbalanced panel, and data for every year of data collection excludes NTMs that were in place before that time, unless they are still in force at the time of data collection.

The largest global NTM database, UNCTAD TRAINS, allows a descriptive statistical analysis as well as the estimation of AVEs. The three most common **descriptive indicators are frequency index, coverage ratio and prevalence score.** They are useful to see the incidence of NTMs as policy tools, but they do neither measure the cost of compliance nor the impact on trade. NTMs inventory measures and indicators provide transparency and allow monitoring of regulatory landscapes but are not sufficient for a full understanding of trade restrictiveness.

To illustrate one way of temporal analysis that is possible using TRAINS, the panel dataset has been divided into two periods, from 2012 to 2016 and from 2017 to 2023. The results suggest that though NTMs are largely more widespread, the increase in number or coverage is not always enormous, as sometimes it is believed. This report documents the methodology for this analysis, and also suggests how sensitive these results are to the underlying data used. For example, if the panel were divided into three or four periods, results could be different. Also, representativity of each grouping is relevant for the analysis. The analysis is restricted by data availability.

AVEs are the next step in the analysis as they quantify the impact of NTMs on trade. **AVEs express the trade restrictiveness of an NTM** in percentage terms equivalent to an import tariff or export tax. They simulate the percentage increase in the price of a product resulting from regulatory measures, thus enabling direct comparison between NTMs and tariffs.

UNCTAD and other **researchers have applied the indicators in several publications** to assess the impact of NTMs on trade and sustainable development and gained important insights into (i) how regulatory impact assessments can be conducted and (ii) how NTMs impact trade and economic, social and environmental development. The UNCTAD NTMs hub provides a link to many of these publications.

UNCTAD TRAINS contains NTMs data for about 150 economies and several years as data points. Data comparability is ensured through a strictly standardized data collection methodology developed by UNCTAD. Because TRAINS is an unbalanced panel dataset, **temporal analyses must account for differences in the timing of data collection across economies**. This limits the analytical possibilities, such as time series or panel data analysis. However, data collection efforts are ongoing, with new economies added and existing datasets updated regularly. Recently, UNCTAD has begun exploring artificial intelligence and large language models to further enhance data collection efficiency and quality, while maintaining methodological consistency. This evolution reflects a broader goal: improving both transparency and quantification techniques to better understand how NTMs influence trade and development. High-quality, standardized data—together with robust quantification tools such as descriptive indicators and AVEs—remain freely available for download, along with the underlying granular TRAINS dataset.

The aim is to better understand the design and use of NTMs and to avoid wrong conclusions and policy recommendations from false analysis. Well-crafted regulations can protect public health, safety, and the environment without imposing unnecessary trade costs. Combining descriptive analysis with rigorous quantification fosters constructive policy dialogue and supports evidence-based regulatory reform. In doing so, it can help to ensure that international trade contributes to sustainable and inclusive development.

Chapter IV

Annex

A1. NTM data availability

This information is valid at the time of writing in Summer 2025. Data is continuously being uploaded as it becomes available. Please check the link below for updated data. https://trainsonline.unctad.org/dataAvailabilityYears

Economy name	Economy code	Economy ISO	2025	2024	2023	2022	2021	2020	2019	2018	2017	2016	2015	2014	2013	2012
Afghanistan	004	AFG														Y
Algeria	012	DZA						Y				Y				
Antigua and Barbuda	028	ATG										Y				
Argentina	032	ARG	Y*	Y	Y	Y	Y	Y	Y	Y	Y	Y	Y	Y	Y	Y
Armenia	051	ARM							Y							
Australia	036	AUS	Y*			Y						Y	Y			
Azerbaijan	031	AZE								Y						
Bahamas	044	BHS											Y			
Bahrain	048	BHR						Y					Y			
Bangladesh	050	BGD									Y					
Barbados	052	BRB											Y			
Belarus	112	BLR									Y					
Benin	204	BEN												Y		
Bolivia (Plurinational State of)	068	BOL	Y*	Y	Y	Y	Y	Y	Y	Y	Y	Y	Y	Y	Y	Y
Botswana	072	BWA			Y						Y					
Brazil	076	BRA	Y*	Y	Y	Y	Y	Y	Y	Y	Y	Y	Y	Y	Y	Y
Brunei Darussalam	096	BRN	Y*							Y			Y			
Burkina Faso	854	BFA														Y
Burundi	108	BDI					Y									
Cabo Verde	132	CPV												Y		
Cambodia	116	KHM	Y*							Y			Y			
Cameroon	120	CMR											Y			
Canada	124	CAN				Y	Y				Y		Y			
Chad	148	TCD					Y									
Chile	152	CHL	Y*	Y	Y	Y	Y	Y	Y	Y	Y	Y	Y	Y	Y	Y
China	156	CHN	Y*									Y				
China, Hong Kong Special Administrative Region	344	HKG										Y				
Colombia	170	COL	Y*	Y	Y	Y	Y	Y	Y	Y	Y	Y	Y	Y	Y	Y
Comoros	174	COM				Y										
Congo	178	COG				Y										
Costa Rica	188	CRI	Y*	Y	Y	Y	Y	Y	Y	Y	Y	Y	Y	Y	Y	Y
Cuba	192	CUB	Y*	Y	Y	Y	Y	Y	Y	Y	Y	Y	Y	Y	Y	Y
Côte d'Ivoire	384	CIV							Y							
Democratic Republic of the Congo	180	COD				Y										
Dominica	212	DMA											Y			
Ecuador	218	ECU	Y*	Y	Y	Y	Y	Y	Y	Y	Y	Y	Y	Y	Y	Y
Egypt	818	EGY										Y				
El Salvador	222	SLV	Y*	Y	Y	Y	Y	Y	Y	Y	Y	Y	Y	Y	Y	Y
Ethiopia	231	ETH											Y			
European Union	918	EUN	Y*		Y	Y	Y	Y	Y	Y		Y	Y	Y	Y	Y
Fiji	242	FJI				Y										
Gabon	266	GAB				Y										
Gambia	270	GMB				Y										
Georgia	268	GEO					Y									
Ghana	288	GHA												Y		
Grenada	308	GRD											Y			
Guatemala	320	GTM	Y*	Y	Y	Y	Y	Y	Y	Y	Y	Y	Y	Y	Y	Y
Guinea	324	GIN					Y									
Guyana	328	GUY											Y			
Honduras	340	HND	Y*	Y	Y	Y	Y	Y	Y	Y	Y	Y	Y	Y	Y	Y
Iceland	352	ISL						Y								

Annex A1. *(continued)*

Economy name	Economy code	Economy ISO	2025	2024	2023	2022	2021	2020	2019	2018	2017	2016	2015	2014	2013	2012
India	356	IND	Y*								Y					
Indonesia	360	IDN	Y*				Y	Y	Y	Y	Y	Y	Y	Y	Y	Y
Israel	376	ISR										Y				
Jamaica	388	JAM											Y			
Japan	392	JPN	Y*			Y						Y	Y			
Jordan	400	JOR										Y				
Kazakhstan	398	KAZ									Y					
Kenya	404	KEN					Y									
Kingdom of Eswatini	748	SWZ				Y										
Korea, Republic of	410	KOR	Y*									Y				
Kuwait	414	KWT						Y								
Kyrgyz Republic	417	KGZ									Y					
Lao People's Democratic Republic	418	LAO	Y*							Y			Y			
Lebanon	422	LBN									Y					
Lesotho	426	LSO				Y										
Liberia	430	LBR												Y		
Malawi	454	MWI			Y						Y					
Malaysia	458	MYS								Y			Y			
Mali	466	MLI												Y		
Mauritania	478	MRT											Y			
Mauritius	480	MUS									Y					
Mexico	484	MEX	Y*	Y	Y	Y	Y	Y	Y	Y	Y	Y	Y	Y	Y	Y
Morocco	504	MAR						Y				Y				
Mozambique	508	MOZ		Y			Y									
Myanmar	104	MMR	Y*			Y				Y			Y			
Namibia	516	NAM				Y										
Nepal	524	NPL														Y
New Zealand	554	NZL	Y*				Y					Y	Y			
Nicaragua	558	NIC		Y	Y	Y	Y	Y	Y	Y	Y	Y	Y	Y	Y	Y
Niger	562	NER					Y									
Norway	579	NOR							Y							
Oman	512	OMN						Y					Y			
Pakistan	586	PAK							Y			Y				
Panama	591	PAN	Y*	Y	Y	Y	Y	Y	Y	Y	Y	Y	Y	Y	Y	Y
Papua New Guinea	598	PNG					Y					Y				
Paraguay	600	PRY	Y*	Y	Y	Y	Y	Y	Y	Y	Y	Y	Y	Y	Y	Y
Peru	604	PER	Y*	Y	Y	Y	Y	Y	Y	Y	Y	Y	Y	Y	Y	Y
Philippines	608	PHL	Y*							Y			Y			
Qatar	634	QAT						Y				Y				
Republic of Türkiye	792	TUR						Y				Y				
Russian Federation	643	RUS						Y				Y				
Rwanda	646	RWA				Y										
Saudi Arabia	682	SAU						Y				Y				
Senegal	686	SEN					Y									
Seychelles	690	SYC				Y										
Singapore	702	SGP	Y*							Y			Y			
Solomon Islands	090	SLB				Y										
South Africa	710	ZAF			Y						Y					
Sri Lanka	144	LKA										Y				
State of Palestine	275	PSE												Y		
Suriname	740	SUR											Y			
Switzerland	757	CHE							Y				Y			
Tajikistan	762	TJK								Y			Y			
Thailand	764	THA	Y*				Y			Y			Y			
Timor-Leste	626	TLS		Y		Y										
Togo	768	TGO				Y										

Annex A1. *(continued)*

Economy name	Economy code	Economy ISO	2025	2024	2023	2022	2021	2020	2019	2018	2017	2016	2015	2014	2013	2012
Trinidad and Tobago	780	TTO											Y			
Tunisia	788	TUN						Y				Y				
Uganda	800	UGA				Y										
United Arab Emirates	784	ARE						Y					Y			
United Kingdom of Great Britain and Northern Ireland	926	GBR								Y		Y	Y	Y	Y	Y
United Republic of Tanzania	834	TZA				Y										
United States of America	842	USA							Y	Y	Y			Y		
Uruguay	858	URY	Y*	Y	Y	Y	Y	Y	Y	Y	Y	Y	Y	Y	Y	Y
Vanuatu	548	VUT				Y										
Venezuela (Bolivarian Republic of)	862	VEN	Y*	Y	Y	Y	Y	Y	Y	Y	Y	Y	Y	Y	Y	Y
Viet Nam	704	VNM	Y*			Y				Y			Y			
Zambia	894	ZMB				Y										
Zimbabwe	716	ZWE		Y							Y					

A2. Panel data divided into two periods

This dumbbell bar figure shows which economies are included in Period 1 and Period 2 for the time analysis in section B.2. There are 45 economies where data has been collected at least once in Period 1 and Period 2 separately.

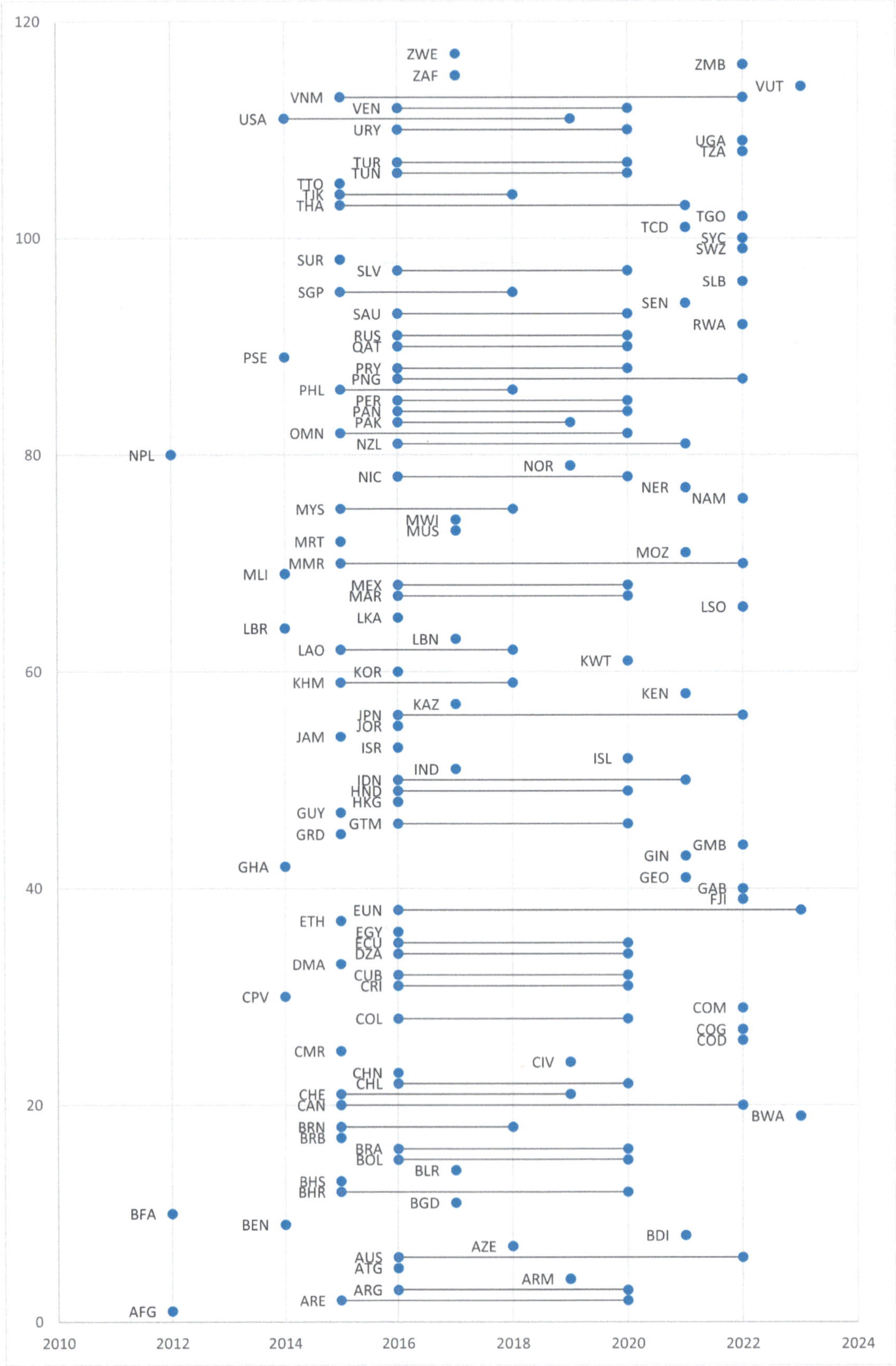

References

Cadot O, Asprilla A, Gourdon J, Knebel C and Peters R (2015). *Deep Regional Integration and Non-Tariff Measures: A Methodology for Data Analysis.* UNCTAD Policy Issues in International Trade and Commodities, Research Study Series No. 69.

Cadot O, Gourdon J and van Tongeren F (2018). *Estimating Ad Valorem Equivalents of Non-Tariff Measures: Combining Price and Quantity Effects*. OECD Trade Policy Papers, No. 215, OECD Publishing, Paris.

Gourdon J (2014). *NTM, Trade and Development: New Data and New Evidence from Africa*. UNCTAD Policy Issues in International Trade and Commodities, Study Series No. 66.

Kee H L, Nicita A and Olarreaga M (2009). Estimating Trade Restrictiveness Indices. *Economic Journal*, Vol. 119, No. 534, pp. 172–199.

Kee H L and Nicita A (2022). Trade fraud and non-tariff measures: An analysis using trade gap estimates. *Journal of International Economics*, Vol. 139, 103682.
Available at: https://doi.org/10.1016/j.jinteco.2022.103682

Nicita A and Gourdon J (2013). *A Preliminary Analysis on Newly Collected Data on Non-Tariff Measures*. UNCTAD Policy Issues in International Trade and Commodities, Study Series No. 53.

Nicita A and Koloskova K (2025). *Non-tariff measures at the border, a GTAP level analysis*. UNCTAD Working Paper #9. - May 2025.

Penello Rial D (2020). *Computing non-tariff measures indicators: analysis with UNCTAD TRAINS Data* - UNCTAD Research Paper No. 41 (UNCTAD/SER.RP/2019/13). Available at: https://unctad.org/publication/computing-non-tariff-measures-indicators-analysis-unctad-trains-data

UNCTAD (2018). *Methodology for the Collection of Non-Tariff Measures: Classification, Data Collection Process and National Experiences*. United Nations publication. UNCTAD/DITC/TAB/2018/3. New York and Geneva.
Available at: https://unctad.org/system/files/official-document/ditctab2018d3_en.pdf

UNCTAD (2019). *International Classification of Non-Tariff Measures*. Available at https://unctad.org/publication/international-classification-non-tariff-measures-2019-version

UNCTAD (2020). Special Topic: Non-Tariff Measures: Estimating Analytical Indicators Using UNCTAD's Trade Analysis Information System (TRAINS). United Nations publication.

UNCTAD (2022). *Non-tariff measures from A to Z*. United Nations publication.

UNCTAD (2023). *Trade Fraud and Non-Tariff Measures*. By Kee, H.L. and Nicita, A. United Nations publication.

UNCTAD (2024). *Non-tariff measures and deep regulatory integration in the African Continental Free Trade Area*. United Nations publication.

UNCTAD (2024a). *Making sense of non-tariff measures: A user's guide to accessing and analysing the data*. United Nations publication.

UNCTAD, World Bank (2018). *The Unseen Impact of Non-Tariff Measures*, United Nations and World Bank.

UNCTAD and WTO (2016). Advanced Guide to Trade Policy Analysis: The Structural Gravity Model. Geneva 2016.

WTO (2012). *World Trade Report 2012: Trade and Public Policies – A Closer Look at Non-Tariff Measures in the 21st Century*. Geneva: World Trade Organization.

The GTAP 11 Satellite Database on Ad-Valorem Equivalents of Border Non-Tariff Measures. Available at: https://www.gtap.agecon.purdue.edu/resources/res_display.asp?RecordID=5111. Based on Kee and Nicita (2022) and consistent with GTAP version 11 Data Base (Aguiar et al., 2022). Data sourced from UNCTAD TRAINS NTM database: trainsonline.unctad.org.